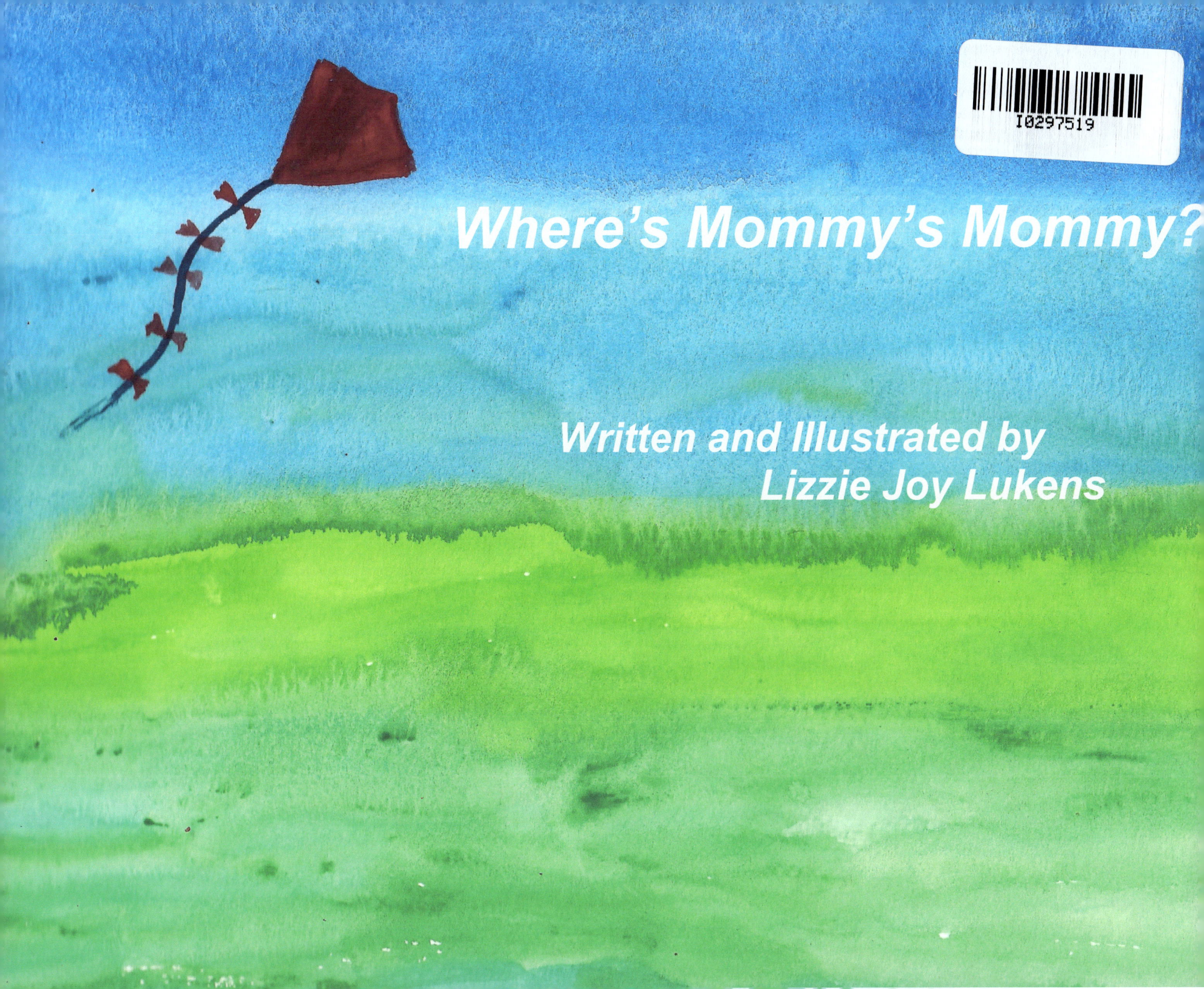

Where's Mommy's Mommy?

Written and Illustrated by Lizzie Joy Lukens

Copyright © 2017 by Lizzie Joy Lukens
All rights reserved. This book or any portion thereof
may not be reproduced or used in any manner whatsoever
without the express written permission of the publisher
except for the use of brief quotations in a book review.

Printed in the United States of America

First Printing, 2017

ISBN 978-0-692-97943-3

Chromis Publications

Dedicated to my mother Kathi, and my Grandma Lukens, and my Grandma Rosie.

May I love my little ones as much as you loved me.

"Where's Mommy's Mommy?"

"*Where is my Mommy?*

She drifted from earth *to heaven before you were born.*"

"Where is Heaven, Mommy?"

"It is both a breath away,

and beyond the stars."

"I once was a little girl like you. My mom and I would build towers with blocks and dream of castles in the sky, just like you and I do now."

"I remember my Grandma. She always had a smile in her eye and a treat in her freezer. She told me stories about what my mommy was like as a little girl."

*"I miss my mom.
Sometimes I still feel sad when I think of her."*

"My mommy wanted to be your grandma.
And now, from heaven, your grandma loves you.

"She is in the sunrise, that leaped for joy when you were born."

*She is in the moon rise,
that sings your dreams in silent lullabies.*

*She is in the rainbow,
that laughs when you smile.*

*She is in the snow,
that dances winter kisses on your cheek.*

She is in the rain that falls when you weep to gently wash away your tears.

*She is in the wind,
that whispers I adore you.*

*Little child of mine,
know you are cherished from afar.*

Rosanna, Paloma, and Zamira,
No book could express the stories my heart holds about your grandparents. You are my deepest joy and their fondest treasure.

Carolyn and Brian,
Grandma Carolyn and Grandma Valerie were such special mothers. Daddy and Mommy wish you could have met them, but we know your grandmothers love you just as much as if they were here with all of us.

Davia Vi,
I cannot put into words how much Grandma Sharon adored you! I hope you always carry her Beauty, Grace, Humor and Love in your life.

www.ingramcontent.com/pod-product-compliance
Lightning Source LLC
Chambersburg PA
CBHW041326290426

44110CB00004B/149